WOW

Working on Wonderful

Inspiration for a Wonderful Life
Volume Two

R.J. OConnor

www.wowrjo.com

WOW
Working on Wonderful

Inspiration for a Wonderful Life
Volume Two

ICR Publishing
Jacksonville, Florida

ISBN 13: 979-8-218-03834-2

LCCN: 2015920206
KDP Publishing
North Charleston, South Carolina

Printed in the United States of America
2022 – First Edition

W.O.W.
Working on Wonderful
Inspiration for a Wonder-filled Life

WOW
Working on Wonderful

Preface

A fantastic life awaits — a life filled with wonder.

In these pages are thoughts that have ignited wonder in my own heart and mind.

The WOW series, Working on Wonderful, is a collection of life reflections. Each represents a moment when life has stopped me, caused me to pause, and inspired me. Life must never be taken for granted. It is constantly reaching out, beckoning to be noticed for the miraculous thing it is.

Some of these thoughts will speak to you. You will have a couple of different ways you can respond. They may inspire you, for instance, to write down your own wonderful thoughts. The back of each page gives you a place to do that. Or you may want to color a page. You may even wish to cut one of your creations from the book and frame it. Or you may wish simply to browse the thoughts without doing either of these things. This book is for you to use as you see fit.

If even one inspires you, then you are further along your way to a wonder-filled life.

I wish you deep, abounding love.
It is my highest hope for you.
When beauty surrounds,
when gratitude resounds,
when magic astounds,
deep love abounds.
— R.J. OConnor

WOW

Working on Wonderful

Add your inspiration.

To the wise,
the little things
are the big things.
- R.J. OConnor

WOW
Working on Wonderful

Add your inspiration.

Life is too serious to
be serious all the time.
Life is too severe to judge
things that happen severely.
Life is too lovely to respond
with anything but love.

- R.J. OConnor

WOW
Working on Wonderful

Add your inspiration.

One person's mole hill
is another's mountain.
Each of us has our own
summit to scale,
but the task is the same.
Climb.
         - R.J. OConnor

WOW

Working on Wonderful

Add your inspiration.

Many have thought about
the vows they have taken
and the honest intention to
honor them.
And the failures.

We ask ourselves now what
it meant and what place those
vows and failures had in the
evolution
of our sacred selves.

Many will stuff the failures
in the Closet of Shame. But
the brave will keep them
in plain view and challenge
themselves to embrace the
brokenness, and in
the embracing,
to find redemption.

                    - R.J. OConnor

WOW
Working on Wonderful

Add your inspiration.

It is cruel to break
someone's spirit, to cause
them to doubt their instinct
to trust. Their willingness to trust
again may be compromised forever.

- R.J. OConnor

WOW

Working on Wonderful

Add your inspiration.

Kindness is a flow through commodity.
It is not something we keep to ourselves.

- R.J. OConnor

WOW
Working on Wonderful

Add your inspiration.

Do not fear being wrong.
This paralyzing dread is stoked by
the judgment of others.
It is pure poison.

- R.J. OConnor

WOW

Working on Wonderful

Add your inspiration.

There is something
about advancing age
that draws us back,
tugs at us relentlessly,
bothers us with
remembrances of the past,
tortures us with
every misstep, every
wrong turn, and
each ill-fated decision.
As the future diminishes
before us, and the
finish line, the date
and time of our flight,
approaches, the past
lengthens before us,
demanding some irrational
reckoning, some
satisfaction or resolution,
a decision whether it
was a good life or a
collection of
squandered years.
Who would have
imagined a crescendo
so discordant, a
misery so grand
and devastating,
this near to
Heaven's gate?
- R.J. OConnor

WOW

Working on Wonderful

Add your inspiration.

Who wants an unscented flower?
Who wants to listen to
a tune with no beat?
Who wants a life with
no spark or glitter
or out-of-breath laughter?

- R.J. OConnor

WOW

Working on Wonderful

Add your inspiration.

Look for who, not what.
- R.J. OConnor

WOW

Working on Wonderful

Add your inspiration.

Some of the things
you've been counting,
don't.
- R.J. OConnor

WOW
Working on Wonderful

Add your inspiration.

Music adds
magic to
words and
soul to their
message.
- R.J. OConnor

WOW

Working on Wonderful

Add your inspiration.

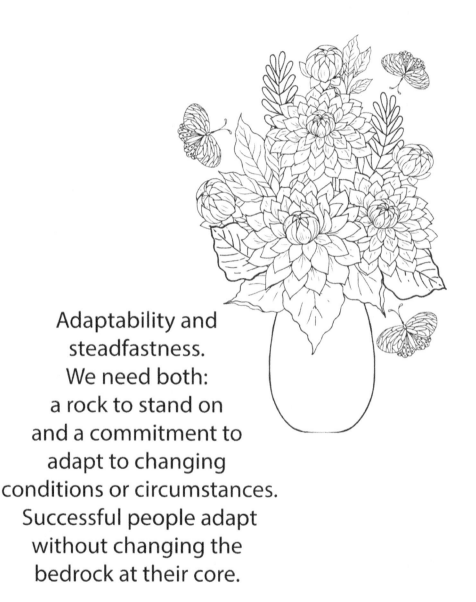

Adaptability and
steadfastness.
We need both:
a rock to stand on
and a commitment to
adapt to changing
conditions or circumstances.
Successful people adapt
without changing the
bedrock at their core.

- R.J. OConnor

WOW

Working on Wonderful

Add your inspiration.

I am convinced that the first two things
we will hear in Heaven
are music and laughter.

- R.J. OConnor

WOW

Working on Wonderful

Add your inspiration.

I believe in new beginnings.
- R.J. OConnor

WOW
Working on Wonderful

Add your inspiration.

People can get so
wrapped up in
themselves that they
see in others only
their own reflection.

– R.J. OConnor

WOW

Working on Wonderful

Add your inspiration.

If you are
planning to
do it "when,"
keep in mind that
when is not some
distant moment.
When is always now.

- R.J. OConnor

WOW
Working on Wonderful

Add your inspiration.

I believe in the
resilience of the
human spirit.
- R.J. OConnor

WOW

Working on Wonderful

Add your inspiration.

I believe in love,
abundant, abounding,
and everlasting.
- R.J. OConnor

WOW

Working on Wonderful

Add your inspiration.

You are only old when adding up
the number of years since
you were born.
How different others see it.
To the very elderly,
you are still young.
To the young, you are ancient.
To the universe,
you are a newborn.
And to God, you are ageless.

- R.J. OConnor

WOW

Working on Wonderful

Add your inspiration.

We behave today as if we can control every tomorrow. But some tomorrows arrive with a reality so unexpected and unrecognizable that we see control as the fantasy it has always been.
- R.J. OConnor

WOW

Working on Wonderful

Add your inspiration.

Core wounds are bone deep
and soul wounding.
There is recovery, eventually,
but never full healing and restoration.
Powerful, terrible,
and yet transformational stuff.
- R.J. OConnor

WOW

Working on Wonderful

Add your inspiration.

There will be time.
My mind will always be sharp.
My energy will always be abundant,
and my resilience will be sure....
And other lies we tell ourselves,
thinking them true, until the page
is turned and the chapter ends.

- R.J. OConnor

WOW

Working on Wonderful

Add your inspiration.

The secret to flying is to
rise through the resistance,
through the blinding clouds,
and through the buffeting
turbulence.
There's no other way.

- R.J. OConnor

WOW

Working on Wonderful

Add your inspiration.

If you give to others what you most need, even as you give it away, you will attract that very thing to yourself.

- R.J. OConnor

WOW

Working on Wonderful

Add your inspiration.

Great suffering comes
from mistaking our wants for our needs.
- R.J. OConnor

WOW

Working on Wonderful

Add your inspiration.

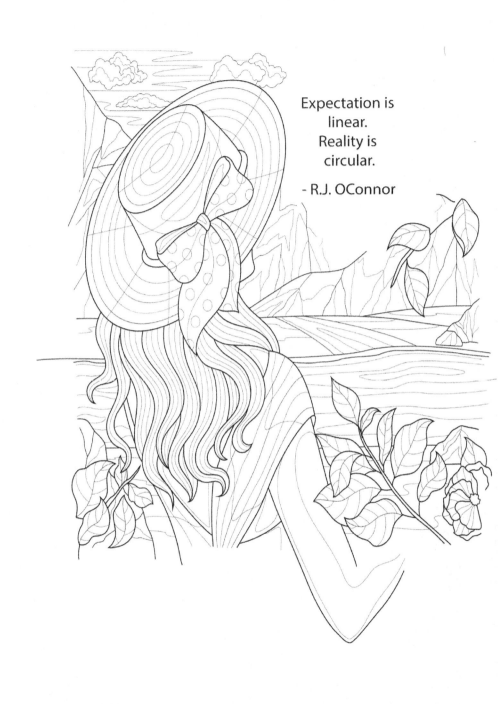

Expectation is
linear.
Reality is
circular.

- R.J. OConnor

WOW

Working on Wonderful

Add your inspiration.

Gratitude is
the pixie dust
of every impossible dream.

- R.J. OConnor

WOW

Working on Wonderful

Add your inspiration.

At the close of each year,
ask yourself this question:
am I a better human
being today than I
was a year ago?

- R.J. OConnor

WOW

Working on Wonderful

Add your inspiration.

Someone will be born today.
Others line up behind them.
Someone will die today and many will crowd
the space behind them, awaiting their turn.
Landings and takeoffs.
They are part of this incredible
thing we call life, and each
arrival and departure
is a sacred moment.

- R.J. OConnor

WOW
Working on Wonderful

Add your inspiration.

Big things.
Little things.
Pressing things.
Urgent things.
What's amazing is the impact
of a sudden illness or loss.
As if by magic,
the picture rearranges.
Big things become small.
Small things become big.
Pressing things are set aside
with no ill effect.
Urgent things are
handled by others.
Life makes space when
illness or tragedy occurs.
Lots of space,
which suggests
it was there all along.

- R.J. OConnor

WOW

Working on Wonderful

Add your inspiration.

Perhaps we must
let the conflict happen,
so that reconciliation can occur.
Because it is
in reconciliation
that bonding occurs.
Like scar tissue,
the broken place
is transformed into something
stronger and it becomes,
in its way,
no less beautiful.

- R.J. OConnor

WOW
Working on Wonderful

Add your inspiration.

Cognizance of what
remains to be known
is intellectual
advancement.

- R.J. OConnor

WOW

Working on Wonderful

Add your inspiration.

As you continue to do
deep work at the soul level,
the outer self begins to
mirror the inner self.
The artificial shell you've worn
to ward off pain and exposure of
our inner torment,
is no longer adequate.
It falls away
and the authentic you
is revealed.
The world has waited for you,
and you've worked your
way to this moment
in the light.

– R.J. OConnor

WOW

Working on Wonderful

Add your inspiration.

What separates us from one another,
and how we judge
each other's success
or failure, is sometimes
nothing more than where
the decimal point sits
on a spreadsheet.
How sad that we judge
each other's lives this way.

– R.J. OConnor

WOW

Working on Wonderful

Add your inspiration.

Empathy is power.
When people disappoint us,
we are tempted to abandon
the sword of empathy in favor
of the twig of resentment.
Hold fast to your strength, dear one.
Let no one rob you
of your power.

- R.J. OConnor

WOW
Working on Wonderful

Add your inspiration.

"Next time"
is not an action statement.
It's a hope, a wish.
"This time"
is the action
statement.

- R.J. OConnor

WOW

Working on Wonderful

Add your inspiration.

The devil may be in the details,
but so is excellence.
Attention to details others neglect yields
excellence others fail to attain.

- R.J. OConnor

WOW

Working on Wonderful

Add your inspiration.

Arrogance makes you stupid.
When you're arrogant,
you stop thinking.
- R.J. OConnor

WOW
Working on Wonderful

Add your inspiration.

Some things cannot
be fixed.
Some things
just are.

– R.J. OConnor

WOW
Working on Wonderful

Add your inspiration.

You are more than you appear to be,
and you are better than you behave.
– R.J. OConnor

WOW

Working on Wonderful

Add your inspiration.

Power
carries the potential to
dehumanize those who
perceive themselves to be powerful.
When people assume a role,
or attain a
professional status, some lose
the compassionate
heart and generous spirit
that once was so much
a part of them.
What robs them of
it now that they have
attained their their status?
It leaves them
less aligned with the
goodness that
makes life impactful.
- R.J. OConnor

WOW

Working on Wonderful

Add your inspiration.

The best platform from which
to launch a wonderful life
is the one you build
with gifts given to other people.

– R.J. OConnor

WOW

Working on Wonderful

Add your inspiration.

Some thoughts will give
me no rest until I
have raised their sails,
tested the winds,
and sent them
on their journey.

– R.J. OConnor

WOW

Working on Wonderful

Add your inspiration.

There is a higher road that
waits for your feet,
and for mine.
– R.J. OConnor

WOW

Working on Wonderful

Add your inspiration.

I believe in happily ever after.
- R.J. OConnor

WOW

Working on Wonderful

Add your inspiration.

Be the Star that says,
"The amount of
darkness surrounding
me has nothing to
do with my decision
to shine."

- R.J. OConnor

WOW

Working on Wonderful

Add your inspiration.

Authenticity awaits:
but be ready to
work like hell to release
the heaven within.
- R.J. OConnor

WOW

Working on Wonderful

Add your inspiration.

Narcisists can look directly at you,
but they see only themselves.

- R.J. OConnor

WOW

Working on Wonderful

Add your inspiration.

There is no such thing as spoiling a dog.
The best you've got is the least they deserve.

- R.J. OConnor

WOW

Working on Wonderful

Add your inspiration.

The gift justifies the pain of its birth.
- R.J. OConnor

WOW

Working on Wonderful

Add your inspiration.

The gift that is locked within -
for whatever reason
it has been locked within -
is miraculous when it is loosed.

- R.J. OConnor

WOW

Working on Wonderful.

Add your inspiration.

Work with the wind.
When the wind is in sync with you,
it is a breeze that is enjoyable and luscious.
When it is against you,
it is something that you must battle through.
When it's coming across you,
it can blow you off course.
When it is behind you,
it can carry you forward.
The more you understand and cooperate,
the less you will be buffeted.
- R.J. OConnor

WOW

Working on Wonderful

Add your inspiration.

Take in the new day
one breath at a time.
Each breath is fresh life.

- R.J. OConnor

WOW

Working on Wonderful

Add your inspiration.

Love means sending
emotional charity and
a warm embrace to the
ickiest of the blickeys.
If we cannot do that,
let us not deceive
ourselves into
believing
we are loving.
- R.J. OConnor

WOW
Working on Wonderful

Add your inspiration.

Many people who judge you
do not see you at all.
When they look at you, they see themselves.
At the root of every judgment is a mirror.

- R.J. OConnor

WOW
Working on Wonderful

Add your inspiration.

"I am so rich," the man said.
"But you have nothing," the boy replied.
"Look again," the man said.
"What am I looking for?" the boy said.
"It's not what," the man said. "It's who."
                                    - R.J. OConnor

WOW
Working on Wonderful

Add your inspiration.

Some lessons are handed to us.
Others are hammered out
on the anvil of our soul.

- R.J. OConnor

WOW

Working on Wonderful

Add your inspiration.

If you get hit in the mouth hard enough,
years later you'll still taste the blood.
- R.J. OConnor

WOW

Working on Wonderful

Add your inspiration.

There's a difference between
going through hell
and going to hell.
Our enemies
wish to send us to hell,
but if we've been
through hell already,
we have the tools
to fight back.

- R.J. OConnor

WOW

Working on Wonderful

Add your inspiration.

Do you want to grow and gain strength?

Or do you want to be safe?

- R.J. OConnor

WOW

Working on Wonderful

Add your inspiration.

What if you wait until
there will be time to do
the thing that makes your
heart beat fast? "Will be"
time is a fiction.

- R.J. OConnor

WOW
Working on Wonderful

Add your inspiration.

Angels are all around us.
They are almost always in disguise.
Some angels are among
us in human form.
Others have four legs.

- R.J. OConnor

WOW

Working on Wonderful

Add your inspiration.

Success is easy
but unattainable for most,
because it requires
muscles we
have not developed:
guts, audacity,
persistence, and a
willingness to work hard.
- R.J. OConnor

WOW
Working on Wonderful

Add your inspiration.

Releasing hold of anger
takes discipline and practice,
but the wise person continually works at it.

- R.J. OConnor

WOW

Working on Wonderful

Add your inspiration.

People who speak
when they don't know
what to say ought to
keep their own counsel
until they do.

- R.J. OConnor

WOW

Working on Wonderful

Add your inspiration.

If I had known how many mistakes
I would make in this life,
I would have apologized upfront.

- R.J. OConnor

WOW

Working on Wonderful

Add your inspiration.

Happiness,
serenity, and self-acceptance
are choices, and
my circumstances
do not deprive me of them.

- R.J. OConnor

WOW
Working on Wonderful

Add your inspiration.

Skip the sightseeing
and site-live in different places,
among different cultures.
Go for a season.
Immerse yourself.

- R.J. OConnor

WOW

Working on Wonderful

Add your inspiration.

Why editing is difficult:
people read their writing
with their own internal autocorrect.
So, the mind will
"see"
what is supposed to be
there instead of what is actually there.

- R.J. OConnor

WOW

Working on Wonderful

Add your inspiration.

I believe in forgiveness
and in the miracle of reconciliation.
- R.J. OConnor

WOW

Working on Wonderful

Add your inspiration.

Maturity requires abandoning one's insistence
on setting one's own rules, and instead
adopting the rules society sets for your behavior.
You adapt and adopt, or you are managed.
Either you manage yourself, or the system will
step in and manage you.
Paradoxically, freedom is the bargaining chip.

- R.J. OConnor

WOW

Working on Wonderful

Add your inspiration.

The reason people's
opinions of us does not matter
is because they do not know us.
The reason we let it matter,
and believe peoples' opinions
about us, is that
we do not know ourselves.

- R.J. OConnor

WOW

Working on Wonderful

Add your inspiration.

We have swollen privilege
and a shriveled heart.

- R.J. OConnor

WOW

Working on Wonderful

Add your inspiration.

If your politics makes
you less human,
is it progress you seek?
                    - R.J. OConnor

WOW

Working on Wonderful

Add your inspiration.

Wisdom is the way of detachment. As they age, the sages pry loose from their attachment to one thing after another until at last they are free.

- R.J. OConnor

WOW

Working on Wonderful

Add your inspiration.

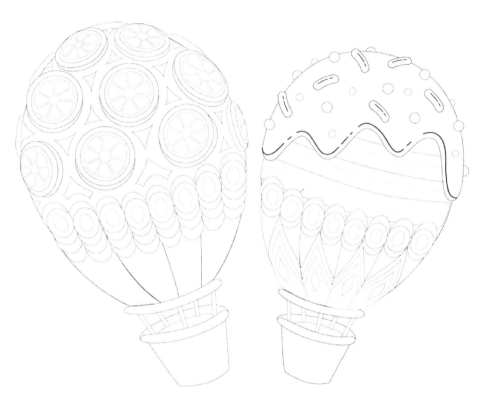

We are like great hot air balloons,
and our attachments are the
anchor ropes. As we untie each
one, we come closer and closer
to flight.

- R.J. OConnor

WOW

Working on Wonderful

Add your inspiration.

All you can do is the best you can do.
There is nothing beyond that, except rest.
- R.J. OConnor

WOW
Working on Wonderful

Add your inspiration.

The person who has a
trusted friend
never walks alone.

- R.J. OConnor

WOW

Working on Wonderful

Add your inspiration.

When you rub a pearl against
your teeth, the fake ones feel
smooth and the real ones
feel rough.
Often, the same is true with people.

- R.J. OConnor

WOW

Working on Wonderful

Add your inspiration.

When it all goes to pieces,
try not to go to pieces with it.
Remember who you are.
- R.J. OConnor

WOW

Working on Wonderful

Add your inspiration.

Forget making lemonade.
When life gives you lemons,
pucker up and kiss each one on its sour cheek.
- R.J. OConnor

WOW

Working on Wonderful

Add your inspiration.

*Be true to yourself and do not
conform to the expectations of
other people. Do not
give into the temptation of
modifying the real you to
seem more acceptable to others.*

- R.J. OConnor

WOW

Working on Wonderful

Add your inspiration.

Easy street doesn't lead to any place I want to go.
- R.J. OConnor

WOW
Working on Wonderful

Add your inspiration.

Some love relationships involve a seismic reversal.
Initially when they want you,
they focus attention on you.
When they have you, the focus shifts
and it's all about them.
Unless one can adapt to that shift,
there will be war.
- R.J. OConnor

WOW

Working on Wonderful

Add your inspiration.

We get jammed up between accepting what is, or
rejecting what is in favor of the change I desire.
Our hearts and minds don't always get it.

- R.J. OConnor

WOW

Working on Wonderful

Add your inspiration.

Happiness comes from knowing
you are a brilliant yellow in a dusk gray world.

- R.J. OConnor

WOW

Working on Wonderful

Add your inspiration.

Love is not limited by space and time.
So if ever you need to be held,
I am already holding you in my heart.

- R.J. OConnor

WOW

Working on Wonderful

Add your inspiration.

Beauty is in the heart of the beholder.

- R.J. OConnor

WOW

Working on Wonderful

Add your inspiration.

When you clear it all away,
a path appears.
Not before.
- R.J. OConnor

WOW

Working on Wonderful

Add your inspiration.

I used to think the worst thing
that could happen to me
is that I would die. It's not.
The worst thing is to feel you've
run out of reasons to keep living.
But having
met that villain in a couple
of dark alleys, I know his
game and refuse to play.

- R.J. OConnor

WOW

Working on Wonderful

Add your inspiration.

Forever is lived a
moment at a time.

- R.J. OConnor

WOW
Working on Wonderful

Add your inspiration.

You are you.
Incomparable.
So do not compare.
- R.J. OConnor

WOW

Working on Wonderful

Add your inspiration.

Of course dreams come true, silly.

- R.J. OConnor

WOW

Working on Wonderful

Add your inspiration.

Delight in the ordinary,
in the little things others take for granted.

- R.J. OConnor

WOW

Working on Wonderful

Add your inspiration.

Time is
the extraordinary gift
denied to many.

- R.J. OConnor

WOW

Working on Wonderful

Add your inspiration.

It is not enough to tie up loose ends.
Some need to be cauterized so
they can never attach themselves to you again.

- R.J. OConnor

WOW

Working on Wonderful

Add your inspiration.

I used to play with matches.
Now I play with words.
There is a striking similarity.

- R.J. OConnor

WOW

Working on Wonderful

Add your inspiration.

Play is work before
it puts on its
grown-up pants.

- R.J. OConnor

WOW

Working on Wonderful

Add your inspiration.

Everyone is in disguise.
Some wear the clown costume,
some the magistrate's robe,
and some the power suit.
All are playing a role
and hiding what's real to do so.

\- R.J. OConnor

WOW

Working on Wonderful

Add your inspiration.

All learning is
positively and
negatively
inspired.
- R.J. OConnor

WOW

Working on Wonderful

Add your inspiration.

You are quick
to tell me
what you hate.
I would like to hear
what you love.
- R.J. OConnor

WOW

Working on Wonderful

Add your inspiration.

Every person is a book,
and the best of them
speak volumes.

- R.J. OConnor

WOW

Working on Wonderful

Add your inspiration.

There are markers of strength,
and resilience is chief among them.
Do you get back up?

- R.J. OConnor

WOW

Working on Wonderful

Add your inspiration.

One of the things that makes writing painful is you must live in the gap between what you experience creatively and what you can make come alive on the page.

- R.J. OConnor

WOW

Working on Wonderful

Add your inspiration.

Do not write with the reader in mind.
Write the truth
and be clear about it.

- R.J. OConnor

WOW

Working on Wonderful

Add your inspiration.

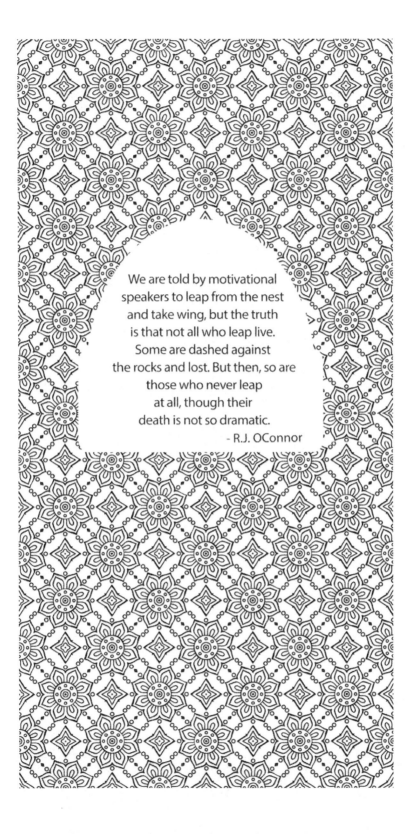

We are told by motivational
speakers to leap from the nest
and take wing, but the truth
is that not all who leap live.
Some are dashed against
the rocks and lost. But then, so are
those who never leap
at all, though their
death is not so dramatic.

- R.J. OConnor

WOW

Working on Wonderful

Add your inspiration.

The moon shines at night
because our darkest places need light.
Indeed, they may need it most.

- R.J. OConnor

WOW

Working on Wonderful

Add your inspiration.

The brave speak with softness,
and lead with gentleness,
but their strength is never mistaken
for weakness. Their look manifests
the roar of a mighty lion.

- R.J. OConnor

WOW

Working on Wonderful

Add your inspiration.

More than anything else,
one's quality of life is
determined by perspective and attitude.

- R.J. OConnor

WOW

Working on Wonderful

Add your inspiration.

There are those who force
their hand, and cause
others to fold (whether in a
negotiation or a relationship), and then
there are those who play
out the hand to the end.
What feels like the greater power play,
is not.

- R.J. OConnor

WOW

Working on Wonderful

Add your inspiration.

Revenge says,
"do unto others as they
have done unto you."
Love says,
"do unto others as you would
want them to do unto you."
Karma says,
"you keep right on loving, and
I will take care of those jokers for you."

- R.J. OConnor

WOW

Working on Wonderful

Add your inspiration.

Priority
plus purpose
plus plan
equals prosperity.

- R.J. OConnor

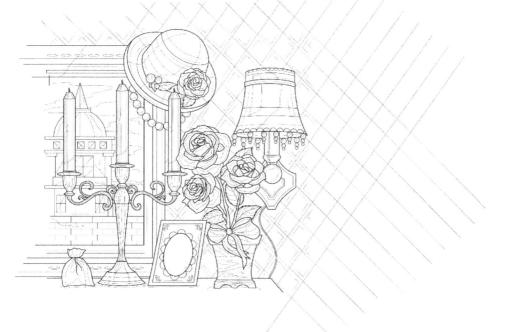

WOW

Working on Wonderful

Add your inspiration.

The Victor,
the Villain,
the Hero,
& the Victim.
If we live a full enough life,
we will have been all of them.

- R.J. OConnor

WOW

Working on Wonderful

Add your inspiration.

Life is such wonderful theater.
Reality isn't at all
what we think it is.

- R.J. OConnor

WOW

Working on Wonderful

Add your inspiration.

Writing fiction is like
living in a parallel universe
and being present in both.

- R.J. OConnor

WOW
Working on Wonderful

Add your inspiration.

People who say they are too busy for you
are sending one of several messages.
1.They are genuinely busy.
Or:
2. They don't prioritize you.
People make time for their top priorities.
Always.
3. They are grabbing power from you,
attempting to diminish you to their level or
below.
4. They are stringing you along.
They want to keep you marginally connected,
but make no mistake about where you stand.
You stand on the margin.
5. Chances are they haven't thought
about you until the moment you
prompted their utterance, "I've been so busy."

- R.J. OConnor

WOW

Working on Wonderful

Add your inspiration.

The good thing about a capsized sailboat
is that it is still a boat.
It can sail again.

- R.J. OConnor

WOW

Working on Wonderful

Add your inspiration.

It is important to love all of yourself.
Love is the only thing that fixes
the things in us that are broken.

- R.J. OConnor

WOW
Working on Wonderful

Add your inspiration.

For all our sophistication,
everyone still poops.
- R.J. OConnor

WOW

Working on Wonderful

Add your inspiration.

The secret to beginning,
and to defeating
procrastination,
is being willing at first
to do it badly.

- R.J. OConnor

WOW

Working on Wonderful

Add your inspiration.

To do something great,
you must be willing
to do one hard thing after another
with no expectation that it will get easier.

- R.J. OConnor

WOW

Working on Wonderful

Add your inspiration.

Simple is lovely. Small is precious.
Less is plenty. Gentle is strong.
Happiness is everywhere.
- R.J. OConnor

WOW

Working on Wonderful

Add your inspiration.

*One day, even this season
of your life will seem hilarious.
Get a jump on the laughter.*

- R.J. OConnor

WOW

Working on Wonderful

Add your inspiration.

You may feel lonely,
but you are never alone.
Believe it,
even if all your senses fail you.

- R.J. OConnor

WOW

Working on Wonderful

Add your inspiration.

Do not fear the sound
of your own voice.
Do not wince at the ring
of your truth.
Only you can speak
the way you do
and impart the truth
given to you.

- R.J. OConnor

WOW

Working on Wonderful

Add your inspiration.

Elements that influence
my quality of life:
1. My attitude.
2. My thoughts.
3. My words.
4. My perspective.
5. My adaptability to
change.

      - R.J. OConnor

WOW

Working on Wonderful

Add your inspiration.

Gentle is the new tough.
- R.J. OConnor

WOW

Working on Wonderful

Add your inspiration.

A great tragedy is the heart
that remains broken
when its destiny
was to heal.

- R.J. OConnor

WOW

Working on Wonderful

Add your inspiration.

Love your deficits.
Strut your limp.

- R.J. OConnor

WOW

Working on Wonderful

Add your inspiration.

I do not hold you to a standard of perfection,
and you mustn't hold yourself to one either.
Imperfect and flawed makes you
no less precious,
and infinitely more interesting.
- R.J. OConnor

WOW
Working on Wonderful

Add your inspiration.

Much like riding a bike
while building it,
we must rest
while we are learning to rest.

- R.J. OConnor

WOW

Working on Wonderful

Add your inspiration.

Even when the storms come,
the sun breaks through
because I carry
my own sunshine.

- R.J. OConnor

WOW

Working on Wonderful

Add your inspiration.

Just because there is a
scientific explanation does
not mean that there isn't a
spiritual reason behind it.

- R.J. OConnor

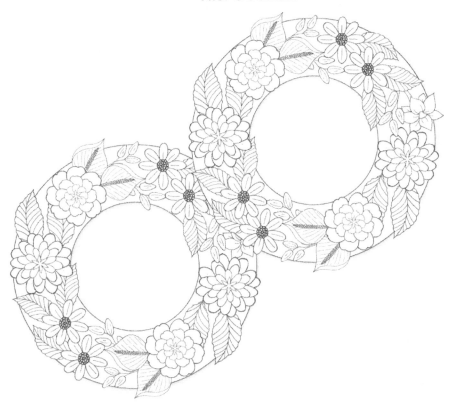

WOW

Working on Wonderful

Add your inspiration.

Given that humiliation
is one of our greatest
fears, it's shocking
how many people
criticize others because
criticising another
humiliates the critic first.

- R.J. OConnor

WOW
Working on Wonderful

Add your inspiration.

Most criticism of others
is self-revelatory and seldom
concerns the one being criticized.
- R.J. OConnor

WOW

Working on Wonderful

Add your inspiration.

Bravery means different things
to different people. Each of us
must decide how
we are being challenged to rise.
- R.J. OConnor

WOW

Working on Wonderful

Add your inspiration.

We need reassurance.

Reassurance that
we will be remembered
after we've gone, perhaps for
a mark we've made,
a life we touched,
or an offering
that mattered.

Reassurance that our brief
measure of years made some
difference to the world.

- R.J. OConnor

WOW
Working on Wonderful

Add your inspiration.

What people think about
you, and what they decide
about you, is their story.

What you choose to think
about yourself, and what you decide
about you, becomes your story.
It is critical to your well-being
to be clear
whose story is whose.

- R.J. OConnor

WOW

Working on Wonderful

Add your inspiration.

If your love
has not matured
into acceptance,
then it is not love.
It is something
less.

- R.J. OConnor

WOW
Working on Wonderful

Add your inspiration.

Appreciation is deep love.
Acceptance is even deeper love.
And public admiration is one of its
obvious manifestations.
Do they boast about you?

- R.J. OConnor

WOW

Working on Wonderful

Add your inspiration.

You are free.
The bondage you may feel is your own doing.
The chains are in your own hands.
You can make other decisions.
Right now. In this moment.
With your next breath.

- R.J. OConnor

WOW

Working on Wonderful

Add your inspiration.

Overheard someone say,
"I remember when
Mike was dying ...."
My thought: was
there ever a moment when
Mike was not dying?

Every day we are living,
we are also dying.
To be living is also to be dying.
Our language denies the reality
but does not alter it.

- R.J. OConnor

WOW

Working on Wonderful

Add your inspiration.

Never judge a visionary
by their early progress, or lack thereof.

- R.J. OConnor

WOW

Working on Wonderful

Add your inspiration.

Failure is the sand that
both spawns the pearl
and refines it.
It is the grist and substance of beauty.
Without failure,
wisdom is more elusive
and art rings hollow.
Failure elicits a pain response,
to be sure. But it also elevates the
human spirit to a place where
hope becomes a possibility
and where peace arrives
as a prize well earned.

- R.J. OConnor

WOW
Working on Wonderful

Add your inspiration.

Unless you risk being
offensive to some,
it will be difficult
to be influential with others.

- R.J. OConnor

WOW

Working on Wonderful

Add your inspiration.

Pain is the great equalizer.
No matter how rich,
how poor, how famous,
or how anonymous you are,
pain levels you
with everyone else.
And in those moments,
we glimpse our common humanity.

- R.J. OConnor

WOW

Working on Wonderful

Add your inspiration.